Oblates

life with St. Benedict

by

Dom Augustine Morris
Monk of Elmore Abbey

Illustrations by Norman Davey
Benedictine Oblate and Architect to the Community

ELMORE ABBEY

1992

Published by Elmore Abbey © 1992

Elmore Abbey, Church Lane, Speen,
Newbury, Berkshire. RG13 1SA

Copies available at the above address.

ISBN 0 9519354 0 2 OBLATES – Life with St Benedict. (pbk).

All quotations are taken from the New English Bible © 1970
by permission of Oxford and Cambridge University Presses

Quotations from the Rule of St Benedict (RB 1980) Copyright © (1980) by
The Order of St Benedict, Inc. Published by
The Liturgical Press, Collegeville, Minnesota. Used with permission.

Printed by Bocardo Press Limited, Didcot.

CONTENTS

PREFACE
By the Abbot of Elmore

What is an oblate? This is an increasingly intriguing question, being asked by a growing number of ordinary folk. The answer is that an oblate belongs to a monastic community and has a share in its life, according to the calling of the individual. It differs only from the life of a monk or nun by degree, for the oblate rule of life, which varies from individual to individual, is based on the monastic rule of St Benedict. It involves being linked to a particular community which is seen as a spiritual home of an extended community, which is united in a common discipline of prayer with the resident community. The resident and the extended community form the confraternity.

OBLATES – LIFE WITH ST BENEDICT is written primarily for the confraternity of oblates belonging to Elmore Abbey, the home of its author. But, as will quickly be discovered, its appeal will be much wider than that. During the past quarter of a century or so, when monastic life itself has seen its enduring qualities and values increasingly questioned, it is the oblate confraternity that has been the growth area. This book will explain this strange phenomenon and give guidance to those seeking to follow the way of stability, conversion and obedience advocated by the rule of St Benedict.

Renewal begins with examination of roots, rediscovering the inspiration and vision of founders. This, of course, takes us to the very heart of the Gospel and from there leads us to look again at the particular charism of the community. In the case of Elmore this is of particular interest. Its first abbot, Father Denys Prideaux, was, we are told, a very reluctant monk and an even more reluctant leader as abbot. He was nothing if not loyal and obedient, and simply did what others told him he ought to do; and so he did, and we remain grateful to him for his fortitude in the face of much discouragement in very difficult times. The truth is that he was a Benedictine oblate by choice, and, given his way, that is what he would most probably have remained. It is not altogether surprising, therefore, that the Elmore confraternity of oblates, both men and women from all walks of life, and including many clergy, has grown from about sixty in the mid 1960's to three hundred and fifty today; and the signs are that the growth is continuing.

I commend this manual for oblates to all who have caught the vision of St Benedict and wish to be pupils in the 'school of the Lord's service', and to others who might be so inspired.

Dom Basil Matthews OSB
March 1992

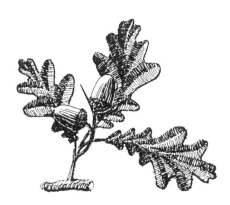

AUTHOR'S FOREWORD

This book is offered to the oblates of our community as a handbook to which they can frequently turn. It does not take the form of a commentary on the Rule of Our Holy Father Benedict, but makes constant reference to the Rule. For the principal purpose of the book is to show how the Rule may be applied in their lives as oblates.

Such is its primary purpose, which is borne in mind throughout. Should it also prove useful to others who regard Benedict as a spiritual guide, that is an additional blessing. As for the more personal details natural in a book for use by the family, it is hoped that such other readers, especially oblates and members of fraternities of other communities, will in their reading supply at such points similar details from their own experience and that of their communities.

Quotations from the Bible are from the New English Bible. Those from the Rule of Saint Benedict are from RB 1980, The Liturgical Press, Collegeville, Minnesota, USA. This translation is divided into verses similar to those of the Bible. This makes it possible to give precise references by chapter and verse. It is hoped that users of other translations will have no difficulty in finding the quotations.

There remains the pleasant duty of expressing gratitude. "I can never thank God enough," said Blessed Maria Gabriella of Unity. Among earthly benefactors, I am specially grateful to the monks of my own community, past and present, particularly to my Abbot, Dom Basil Matthews, for contributing the preface and for his constant support and encouragement; to my predecessor as oblate master, Dom Godfrey Stokes; and to those monks and oblates who have aided by criticism and suggestion. To them all, and to innumerable others, the backroom girls and boys who support us by friendship and prayer, my heartfelt thanks and promise of remembrance before the sole Author of all that is good.

Augustine Morris

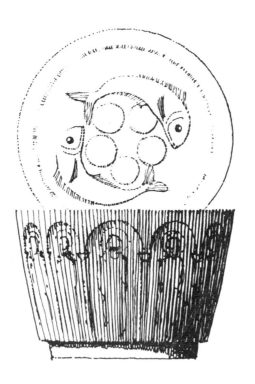

CHAPTER ONE:

The Meaning and Purpose of Oblateship

WHAT IS AN OBLATE?

It is common practice for a Religious Community such as ours to be surrounded by an inner group of friends who have a special link with the Community; an Association, a Fraternity, or whatever title may be given to this inner group. Broadly speaking, such groups fall into two categories: tertiaries and oblates.

Tertiaries

The name "tertiary" belongs properly to the Franciscans. The tertiaries are, as the name implies, a third order, the first being the friars, the second the sisters, and the third the tertiaries, men and women living outside friaries and convents, but following basically a common rule of life which may be adapted to individual circumstances, and by that common rule constituting themselves as the third order within the Franciscan family.

Oblates

The name "oblate", originally meaning a person who is offered, nowadays signifies one who offers the self to God in association with a monastic Community. Each oblate volunteers to undertake a personal rule of life which takes

1

into consideration the particular circumstances of each, and is then sanctioned by the community. Oblates do not, therefore, constitute an "order" as such. They may nevertheless forge strong links with one another, especially in local groups, in addition to the personal bond which links each with the parent Community.

The Monastery of their Oblation

Benedictine oblates are oblates of a particular community, not of the Benedictine Order as a whole. Further, the monastery of their oblation is a spiritual home, at whatever distance from it they may live. Of the whole family belonging to that house, the Abbot of the monastery is the father, and the oblates as well as the monks are brothers and sisters. It will, however, be normal for the Abbot to depute many of his functions to an Oblate Master, who, on behalf of the Abbot and Community, makes the oblates his special care.

Definition

An oblate is therefore a Christian who is called by God to undertake a disciplined life under rule, in close asociation with a Benedictine monastery such as Elmore Abbey.

WHY BENEDICTINE?

Oblates, as members of the extended family of the monastery, will desire not only to familiarise themselves with the Rule of Saint Benedict (henceforth referred to as RB), under which their brothers the monks live, but also to order their lives in accordance with the spiritual principles enunciated in RB.

RB and the spirituality founded upon it can be characterised as:

1. SCRIPTURAL

Benedict constantly quotes scripture: RB could be said to be a tissue of quotations from the Bible. "What page, what passage of the inspired scriptures of the Old and New Testaments is not the surest of guides for human life?" (RB 73,3). Above all he values the gospels: his monks are to walk "with the gospel for our guide" (RB Prologue 21). Oblates will include in their personal rule a daily reading, however brief, of scripture.

2. LITURGICAL

A large part of the day of the monk is spent in the corporate worship of God, which Saint Benedict calls "the work of God" (RB 58, 7). Oblates' rules will therefore include participation in public worship and the private recitation of some part of the office, in which they unite themselves with the monastic choir. RB lays down no regulations about private prayer or its method: Benedict simply says, "Devote yourselves often to prayer" (RB 4, 56). "If anyone chooses to pray privately, he may simply go in and pray" (RB 52, 4). "Prayer," he says, "should be short and pure, unless perhaps it is prolonged under the inspiration of divine grace" (RB 20, 4). In these more complex days, oblates' rules will include periods of private prayer, and oblates will seek to make an annual retreat.

3. SACRAMENTAL

By this is to be understood not only reception of the sacraments of the church, but also a view of life which seeks to discern beneath and within the outward and visible things their inward and spiritual significance. In this spirit the cellarer of the monastery "will regard all utensils and goods of the monastery as sacred vessels of the altar, aware that nothing is to be neglected" (RB 31, 10,11). Oblates' rules will not only specify the frequency with which each will receive the sacraments, but also a general resolve to live according to this spirit.

4. CORPORATE

RB is constantly concerned about the personal relationships of the monks with one another as well as the Abbot: "to their fellow-monks they show the pure love of brothers; to God, loving fear; to their Abbot, unfeigned and humble love" (RB 72,8–10). In the very varying circumstances of their personal lives, oblates will seek to practise such behaviour in their family, business and personal relationships. Nevertheless, they will also value silence and solitude, and learn the discipline of the tongue (RB 6; also RB 4,25–28 and 51–54).

5. DISCIPLINED

Monks live under vow of obedience to their Abbot, "who is believed to hold the place of Christ in the monastery" (RB 2,2). Such obedience enables them to escape from the self-assertiveness and self-pleasing which otherwise might motivate their conduct. For the like reason, oblates will obey lawful authority in church and state, and will, as may be appropriate to the status and circumstances of each, give effect to the injunction of Benedict: "no-one is to pursue what he judges better for himself, but instead, what he judges better for someone else" (RB 72,7).

4

6. ORDINARY

At the outset of RB, Benedict announces his intention "to establish a school of the Lord's service. In drawing up its regulations, we hope to set down nothing harsh, nothing burdensome." (RB Prologue, 45, 46). For oblates, the "school of the Lord's service" is to be found in the humdrum ordinary duties of life as they present themselves day by day and hour by hour, each moment bringing its own grace from God till the whole is permeated by his love.

Such progress is thus described by Benedict: "As we progress in this way of life and in faith, we shall run in the way of God's commandments, our hearts overflowing with the inexpressible delights of love. Never swerving from His commandments, but faithfully observing His teaching until death, we shall through patience share in the sufferings of Christ that we may deserve to share in His kingdom. Amen" (RB, concluding words of Prologue).

HOW DOES ONE BECOME AN OBLATE?

Personal Contact

It is obvious from what has been said above about the nature of oblateship as a personal link with the community, that the immediate answer to this question is "by personal contact with the monastery and its monks, especially the Abbot and the Oblate Master." Except in the case of the disabled and those living abroad, a preliminary visit to the monastery is therefore essential.

References

Supposing that both sides are happy about such a meeting and that it seems right to proceed, then, with the approval of the Abbot, intending oblates will be asked to provide two references from priests who know them well. They will also be asked to draw up a personal rule of life in accordance with the principles described above, which will be submitted to the Oblate Master, whose advice may be sought in this matter.

Oblate Novice

These preliminaries being settled, arrangements will be made for the applicant to be received as an oblate novice. This ceremony will if possible take place in the monastery in the presence of the monks, the Abbot presiding. The oblate novice will be given a token scapular. The full scapular is the hooded garment which the monks wear over their shoulders; and that given to the oblates therefore betokens the brotherhood into which they are received. The oblate noviceship lasts for a minimum of one year, and provides opportunities for trying out the rule and developing the relationship with the support of the monks and other oblates.

Full Oblates

Oblate novices wishing to proceed to full oblation apply to the Oblate Master, who submits the request to the Abbot and chapter, together with the references already received and a report on the novitiate. If the vote is favourable, arrangements are made for the reception of the oblate promises, over which the Abbot presides, usually at the Conventual Mass. These promises are not vows in the technical sense of that word, equivalent to marriage or religious vows: nevertheless, they are the expression of a serious commitment and resolve on the part of the oblate.

HOW IS CONTACT MAINTAINED?

Oblate Day

Every year on the Saturday following July 11th, the Solemnity of Saint Benedict, Oblate Day is celebrated at Elmore Abbey, when as many oblates as are able to come spend the day at the monastery sharing the worship, instruction, hospitality and friendship of the monks and of their fellow oblates.

Quiet Days

Quiet Days are arranged at Elmore to which all oblates are invited: for these they are invited to bring their own packed lunch. On such occasions, as also on Oblate Day, the community's worship is transferred to the neighbouring Church of St. Mary's, Speen, by kind permission of the Vicar and churchwardens.

Retreat

An annual retreat is arranged elsewhere, conducted by one of the monks. Although all oblates, priests included, are welcome to attend such retreats, preference is give to women oblates, for whom accommodation cannot be provided at the monastery.

Renewal of Promises

It is expected that oblates will renew their promises annually in November, either privately or at a group meeting. Oblates and oblate novices are strongly recommended to make an entry in their diaries for All Saints' Day that they should, in the course of the month, report concerning their observance of their rule to the Oblate Master. He accordingly anticipates that his November mail will be unusually heavy.

London and Provincial Groups

By kindness of the Dean and Chapter of Westminster Abbey, London-based oblates meet there annually in November for Mass celebrated by the Oblate Master with Renewal of Oblation, followed by a buffet supper. In addition, this group meets quarterly for evening Mass and supper. There are various other groups in the provinces which arrange meetings, although by no means is the whole of England covered. The Oblate Master is always glad to assist in making contacts, and it is occasionally possible for one of the monks to attend and speak at such meetings. Elmore oblates are strongly encouraged to make contact with similar groups attached to other communities, whether Anglican or ecumenical.

Oblate Letter

The Oblate Letter is circulated to all oblates, novices included, three or four times a year. It includes news of the community and its oblates and notification of meetings, whether at Elmore or elsewhere, together with material intended for the spiritual sustenance of oblates. It may also include book reviews and suggestions for reading, particularly such as may be relevant to Benedictine life.

Correspondence

Oblates are welcome to maintain contact with the community by visits and correspondence, not only with the Oblate

Master, who, however, has a special responsibility for fostering such friendships. For others living at a distance from the monastery, especially those overseas, such letters are a valued link with their spiritual home.

Above All, Prayer

Beyond all such external contacts is the strong bond of prayer, monks for oblates and oblates for monks and for one another, together with the awareness of sharing a common dedication and a common purpose. The knowledge of this profound and life-giving reality is a source of constant encouragement to every member of the monastic family, not least to the monks themselves.

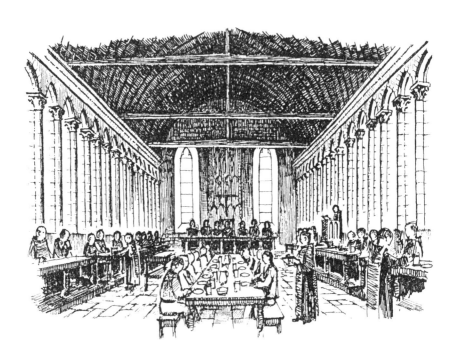

CHAPTER TWO:

Saint Benedict

SOURCES

"Dialogue Two"

Unfortunately, not a great deal can be known with certainty of the life of St. Benedict. Outside RB there is really only one source: the second of the four books of *Dialogues* of Saint Gregory the Great, which is wholly devoted to Benedict. Gregory was writing fifty years after Benedict's death, and his purpose was rather to edify his readers than to record facts. *Dialogue II* is little more than a collection of miraculous events illustrating the supernatural power of God operating through Benedict.

Miracles

In his narrative, Gregory is greatly influenced by incidents recorded in the Bible and in earlier accounts of holy persons. Thus Benedict is presented as "filled with the spirit of all the just," performing miracles reminiscent, for instance, of those of Moses, Elijah and Saint Peter. Benedict had especially the power of foretelling the future, including the prevision of the destruction, after his death, of his own monastery of Monte Cassino, of the knowledge of distant events, and of reading souls. Today we might speak of extra-sensory perception. More attractive, however, are Benedict's interventions on behalf of the poverty-stricken and oppressed. It is likely that a core of truth underlies these narratives.

King Alfred

For all its defects from the point of view of historical research, *Dialogue II* has been important in the spread of Benedictine monasticism. Throughout the Middle Ages, it was the most popular of Gregory's works, and did much to assure Benedict's fame. In our own country, for instance, when King Alfred was labouring to restore the culture of his realm after its devastation by the Danes, he had *Dialogue II* translated into Anglo-Saxon with a view to the revival of the monastic life.

Evidence

Nor can the historical value of Gregory's work be altogether discounted, for he claims to have culled evidence from the successors of Benedict at both Subiaco and Monte Cassino. He also makes incidental references to other persons connected, though distantly, with Benedict's story and known to Gregory from other sources.

A Figure of Significance

It is at least evident that the Pope regarded Benedict as a figure of significance and importance, for no other figure in the *Dialogues* receives comparable treatment. Perhaps the most that can be said is that these were the sort of stories which were in circulation about Benedict half a century after his time. Consequently, they do give us at least some notion of the character and influence of their subject. *Dialogue II* can still be read with pleasure and profit.

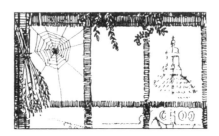

LIFE, DEATH AND CHARACTER
OF BENEDICT

If we say that Benedict was born in AD 480 and died in 547, we are likely to be not far wrong.

Abstracting from the miraculous element in *Dialogue II* we get the following from Gregory:

Early Life

Born of good parentage at Nursia (now Norcia) in central Italy, Benedict was sent to Rome for his education. However, disgusted by the loose morals of his fellow students, he left before completing his course, and set up home with his nurse, who at this point would be better described as his housekeeper. How long this situation continued is uncertain, but it came to an abrupt end when the mending of a sieve was thought to be miraculous and attributed to Benedict's prayers.

A False Start

The event caused such a stir that Benedict went off by himself and found refuge in a cave at Subiaco, where he lived the life of a hermit, befriended and assisted by a monk of a neighbouring monastery. Again we do not know how long his life as a hermit lasted. It came to a temporary end when he agreed, against his better judgement, to be abbot of the monks of Vicovaro. His efforts to impose discipline proved so unpopular that the monks even tried to poison him, and he returned to his cave at Subiaco.

The Real Thing

Now, however, he was joined by men of more serious religious purpose, whom he organised into groups under his presidency. This growth must have taken place over a considerable period of time. But once again he encountered opposition, this time from the jealousy of a local priest who tried to corrupt his monks. (The priest, Florentius, was grandfather to Gregory's subdeacon of the same name).

To Monte Cassino

Benedict decided to leave Subiaco with a few chosen disciples and to settle at Monte Cassino. It may be estimated that he would now be about fifty years old. At Cassino he had first to combat the remains of pagan religion. But there, on the mountain, he built his monastery; there he wrote his Rule; and there, some twenty years later, he died, standing to receive Holy Communion, supported on the arms of his monks.

His Sister

Two incidents which took place before his death deserve mention.The first was the final one of his annual meetings

with his sister Scholastica – her only appearance in *Dialogue II*. She died shortly after her visit to her brother, and Benedict had her body brought to the monastery. It was there interred in the chapel of Saint John the Baptist where his own body was to lie at her side.

In a Sunbeam

The second incident deserving special notice also took place not long before his death: his vision of the whole world gathered into a single sunbeam. This experience of his may call to our mind the later well-known vision of Mother Julian of Norwich of the universe as no larger than a hazel nut. Benedict's experience prompts Gregory to the apt comment that "all creation is small to the soul that sees the Creator."

What Sort of Man?

For more precise knowledge of the character of Benedict, Gregory rightly refers us to his Rule, "for the holy man cannot have taught otherwise than as he lived." Accordingly, we look specially at chapter 64 of RB, where Benedict is describing the qualities to be looked for in the election of an Abbot. It deserves close attention not only for those who would know Benedict, but also as a model for all oblates in positions of responsibility towards others.

Self-Portrait

It is the portrait of a man of firm principles, able to take decisions, but always with consideration for those who will be affected by them; mature enough to deal with details without becoming petty-minded; capable of inspiring high ideals in men engaged in humdrum mundane tasks; sympathetic with their weaknesses of body or character; willing to listen to advice but able to make up his own mind; a leader who seeks "to be loved rather than feared" (RB 64, 15), and is rewarded even in this life by the trust and "unfeigned and humble love" of his monks (RB 72, 10).

THE RULE OF SAINT BENEDICT

A Heritage

There had been monks and nuns in the Christian Church two hundred years before Benedict. Starting among lay Christians in Egypt, the monastic movement had spread rapidly in East and West alike, and was widespread long before his time. As a monk he was entering into a heritage already rich in tradition.

Decadence and Cure

Benedict believed himself to be living in an age of monastic decadence: he had had painful experience of it at Vicovaro. In the first chapter of RB, alongside two good sorts of monks, the hermits who lived alone and the cenobites who lived in community, Benedict describes also two bad sorts, who must have been all too common. But reform was in the air. One of the principal means of securing it would be to embody sound monastic practice in a written Rule.

Another Rule

Benedict was not alone in having recourse to this means: other monastic leaders were engaged in writing monastic Rules in the same period. Of these others, one, whose name is unknown, requires our attention. His Rule is written in dialogue form, the questions of a disciple being answered by a master. Hence it is known as *The Rule of the Master*, RM for short, just as RB is short for Rule of Benedict.

Which was Earlier?

Large portions of RM are word for word the same as RB: especially is this so in the Prologue of RB and its first seven chapters, which are basic to the whole Rule. RM is three times as long as RB, and it was for long thought to be an expansion of Benedict's Rule. But, on the contrary, it is now universally accepted that RM is the earlier of the two, and that it was on Benedict's desk as he wrote.

Fresh Light

At first sight it seems disconcerting to have to admit that RB is not the work of one mind only, but of two. Nevertheless, the discovery throws a great deal of fresh light on Benedict's mind; for we see what of RM he retains, what he discards, what he modifies, and where he writes on his own.

The Same Authority

Comparison between the two Rules can only deepen our appreciation of Benedict's wisdom. More than that: the comparison makes us value all the more Benedict's humanity, his insight into and sympathy with the weaknesses of human nature, alongside its potentialities for good. All that apart, however, the discovery of the priority of RM makes no difference to the validity of RB as it stands. Its teaching throughout, whatever the source of it, retains the same authority.

Thorough Knowledge

One great difficulty about accepting Gregory's account of Benedict's earlier life as recorded in *Dialogue II* is this: it seems to offer no opportunity for access to books. Benedict left Rome, says the Pope, "wisely uneducated." Yet somehow Benedict must have had ample opportunity to gain a thorough knowledge of Scripture and a widespread acquaintance with Christian, especially monastic, literature.

A Great Deal of Reading

When he came to write his Rule, he expected those who would follow it to do a great deal of reading. He bids the monk "listen willingly to holy reading" (RB 4, 55). In addition to the scriptural and other readings in the daily office (RB 9), there is always to be reading aloud at meals (RB 38), and also every evening before Compline (RB 42). Moreover, although the daily timetable varies with the seasons, provision is always made for the monk to spend a considerable portion of every day in private reading (RB 48).

A Remarkable Rule

It is evident from all this that, whatever *Dialogue II* may say about Benedict's youth, there must have been ample opportunity for the future writer of the Rule to read both widely and deeply. For as Gregory himself says, Benedict "was eminent for his teaching, for he wrote a Rule for monks which is remarkable both for its discretion and for the lucidity of its style." Gregory continues, in words already quoted, "the holy man cannot have taught otherwise than he lived." Such an advocate of reading must himself have read much, and RB bears witness to that fact.

A Potent Force

The summary of Benedictine spirituality given above in chapter I indicates that RB is a distillation of traditional Christian wisdom. There is little in it which is original in the sense of never having been said before. Rather it is the distillation itself, through the mind of Benedict, which makes RB a highly original work, stamped with his personality. It is this combination of the traditional with the personal and the practical which has made RB so potent a force in the church and in the world through the fourteen centuries since it was written.

Influential

It has long been realised how greatly western Europe is indebted to Benedict for the rebuilding of its civilisation after the dark ages. Canterbury, Westminster, Durham, and many another name in our land bear witness to his influence in England, the most Benedictine of countries. More recently, the labours of historians and other scholars – and not least monks and nuns among them – have given our generation fresh insights into Benedict's mind. It is safe to say that his reputation never stood higher. He still has much to say to us, and most of all as a guide to Christian living.

CHAPTER THREE:

The Benedictine Family

HOW DID THE RULE SPREAD?

"A Little Rule"

The influence which Benedict has exercised through the Rule he wrote is incalculable. Yet at the time of writing he could have had no intention of founding an order: such an idea would be an anachronism. He is engagingly modest about RB, "a little Rule we have written for beginners" (RB 73, 8).

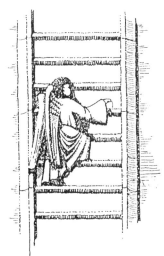

"For Monasteries"

Nevertheless, here and there in the Rule there are indications that Benedict anticipated that it might be observed in other monasteries besides his own. For instance, in his final chapter he writes, "The reason we have written this Rule is that by observing it in monasteries" – notice the plural – "we can show that we have some degree of virtue and the beginnings of monastic life" (RB 73, 1).

To the Centre

As Benedict's prophetic spirit had foreseen, his own monastery of Monte Cassino was doomed to destruction. It was sacked by the invading Lombards some thirty years after his death. By the irony of fate – or ought we not rather to say by the over-ruling Providence of God? – this catastrophe aided the spread of the Rule, for it brought it to the centre of Christendom. The monks took refuge in Rome, bringing the Rule with them. Had it not been for that disaster, it is possible that Gregory would never have heard of Benedict – and maybe nor would we.

The "Law"

As we have seen, others besides Benedict were writing rules for monks, for instance the "Master" before him and the Irish saint Columban after him. Those who write rules expect them to be accepted and obeyed, at least in their own monasteries. Thus Benedict instructs the Abbot to "keep this Rule in every particular." (RB 64, 20). And of the reception of a novice he says, "Let this Rule be read straight through to him, and let him be told, 'This is the law under which you are choosing to serve'" (RB 58, 9,10).

A Way of Life

In spite of these strong expressions about the Rule, it would be an error to adopt a rigorist attitude to RB – or any other of the Rules of that period – as if it were intended as a legal code. Precise though many of its instructions are, RB is not so much a piece of legislation as a description of a way of life. "Way of life" is indeed a favourite figure of Benedict: he loves to see life as a pilgrimage (RB 5, 12), a following of Christ (RB 72, 12), a journey that "leads to God and everlasting life" (RB 72, 2). RB is a guide-book for the pilgrim. It embodies in practical form the principles which should guide Christian life in general and monastic life in particular. It is because Benedict's genius has accomplished this purpose so effectively that his Rule has continued to be followed in the most varying circumstances through the centuries, whereas the Rules of his contemporaries have left little mark in history.

A Handbook

The seal of Gregory's approval certainly counted for something. But it was not by any authoritative stance on his part or that of any other that the use of RB spread in the three centuries following Benedict's death. Benedict had provided a masterly guide to the monastic way of life which other monasteries found useful, and applied as suited their own circumstances. For instance, there was a period in the history of the monastery of Bobbio, an Irish foundation in Italy, when the Rules of Columban and Benedict were observed side by side – to the modern mind an impossible feat, so different are they both in spirit and in practice. Yet it was so, and the fact provides vivid illustration of the attitude of mind to any such Rule, an attitude which sees the Rule not so much as a legally binding code, but rather a handbook, a guide to virtuous living, alongside other such guides.

To England

Pope Gregory's most famous act was his mission in 596 to the Anglo-Saxons. For this he employed forty monks from his own monastery in Rome. Did they bring with them a copy of RB? We do not know, but certainly the Rule was known, appreciated and used in our country not much later. The Anglo-Saxon monks and nuns are certainly rightly counted as sons and daughters of Benedict, though the actual designation ''Benedictine'' did not come into use until very long afterwards. The oldest of the hundreds of manuscripts of RB still existing is in the Bodleian library at Oxford: it is thought to have been copied either at Canterbury or at Worcester towards the end of the seventh century.

Back to Starting Point

From England to Italy in 729 there travelled an Anglo-Saxon monk, Willibald by name. Accustomed as he was to the use of RB in England, Willibald re-introduced it at Monte Cassino which had been refounded a dozen years earlier, but without Benedict's Rule. Thus the debt owed by England to Benedict through Gregory was repaid by an Englishman in the very place where Benedict had penned it two centuries earlier.

To Germany

At much the same time, another English monk was on his way from his native land to Germany, then wholly pagan. This was St. Boniface, apostle of Germany. With the aid of monks and nuns from England, he preached the gospel far and wide, and established monasteries and convents as centres of evangelisation and civilisation. Among his assistants was the aforementioned Willibald, who after ten years at Monte Cassino, was sent by the Pope to aid Boniface and his compatriots. The life of Boniface was crowned by martyrdom, but his work continued, including the spread of Benedict's Rule.

Another Benedict

Benedict of Monte Cassino is not the only saint of that name: another is Benedict of Aniane, also an abbot. In 817 Benedict of Aniane presided over a congress of abbots at Aachen, which attempted to impose uniformity of observance in all the monasteries in the extensive area of western Europe which had come under the sway of Charlemagne. At long last the use of RB was imposed by authority, three centuries after it had been written.

Inconceivable

But the way of monastic life fostered by Benedict of Aniane was a fusion of many other elements with RB. The life lived in the monasteries of the reform differed in many respects from the simplicities of life at Monte Cassino. It was closely integrated into both church and state in a manner which would have been inconceivable in the earlier age.

Loss of Balance

One consequence was the splendour of monastic churches and of the worship offered in them, very different from Benedict's simple "oratory" (RB 52). Another was that, whereas priest-monks had been exceptional at Cassino (RB 60 and 62), now it became increasingly normal for monks to be ordained. The balance between prayer, reading and manual work characteristic of RB was abandoned in favour of a heavy concentration on liturgical worship. And whereas RB, in comparison with RM and other Rules of the period, had substantially diminished the quantity of psalmody, the new monasticism greatly increased it.

Pattern for Centuries

What Benedict of Aniane fostered, or something very like it, became the pattern of monastic life through most of the Middle Ages. When King Alfred's hopes for a revival of monastic life in England after the Danish devastations were finally realised in his grandson's time, this was the pattern it took. And this was the pattern of Benedictine life which from that time on remained effective in England right up to the Reformation. Even in the changed circumstances of today that pattern remains a potent force.

Achievements

It was a pattern which conferred immense benefits on the society into which it was so closely interlinked. It trained able administrators who served both church and state; it preserved for posterity the ancient learning; it fostered education and the arts, music, painting and the allied crafts, and, above all, architecture. Many of our great cathedrals and churches are a heritage from it, a lasting memorial to its glories, whether they are Romanesque or Gothic. Specially is this so of the Gothic buildings, for that style was the brain-child of Abbot Suger of Paris, architect of the Abbey of Saint Denis, the first Gothic church. But above all it produced great saints, Dunstan of Glastonbury and Canterbury, his friends Ethelwold of Abingdon and Winchester and Oswald of Worcester and York; and in a later age, Anselm of Bec in Normandy and of Canterbury and his contemporary Wulstan of Worcester, and many another saintly man and woman, in this country and all western Europe.

Against the Established Pattern

There were reactions within the Middle Ages against this established pattern of monastic life and in favour of a return to the primitive simplicities. Of such reactions the principal one was the foundation of the Cistercian order in the eleventh century. It spread like wildfire, not least in England and Wales; in Ireland it became the predominant form of monastic life. In effect, the Cistercian reform meant that henceforward Benedictine life would flow in two main streams, the "black" and the "white", the Cistercians being the "white" Benedictines. Both alike were living under RB, differently as they interpreted it and applied it. But both alike were swept aside in England and most of Northern Europe by the tide of the Reformation.

THE BENEDICTINE FAMILY TODAY

Strictly speaking, the name "Order of Saint Benedict" is a misnomer, if it is taken to imply a centralised government imposing order from above. The unit is always the individual monastery, although most monasteries today are grouped into "Congregations", associations of monasteries following a common pattern of life. Such Congregations may be either basically national, such as the French Congregation, which is represented in England by the Abbeys of Quarr and Saint Cecilia's, Ryde, on the Isle of Wight; or international, such as the Subiaco Congregation, represented in this country by Ramsgate Abbey and others. Moreover, Cistercian monks and nuns, though separately organised, also follow the Rule of Saint Benedict and are no less his sons and daughters, though not described as O.S.B.

The unit, as has been said, is always the individual monastery, a closely knit community bonded together by what would nowadays be called a strong team spirit. This is a very positive value. But it has its dangers, and these were not escaped by the monasteries of our country in the Middle Ages. All too often, each monastery was only too zealous in defence of what it regarded as its own rights and privileges, against all comers.

Nevertheless, when in the fourteenth century Rome urged the monasteries of different countries to form national associations, it was in England alone that this initiative found lasting response. Today most of the monasteries in our country belong to the English Benedictine Congregation, which claims a direct personal link, though a tenuous one, with the pre-Reformation monks of England. Consequently, among all the Congregations, the English is reckoned senior, next only to Monte Cassino itself.

Anglican Benedictine monks and nuns, all taken together, form a very small proportion of the total family of living Benedictines, of whom by far the greater number are in communion with the see of Rome. Nevertheless, Anglican Benedictines are generously recognised by their Roman Catholic brothers and sisters to have an authentic place within the family.

In 1893 there was held the first Congress of Benedictine Abbots in Rome. It took place at the International College of Sant' Anselmo founded by Pope Leo XIII as a central house of study for young monks. At the head of the College is the Abbot Primate, whose authority in the Order is, however, strictly limited. It may be likened with some justice to that of the British Crown, a focus of unity able to exert a beneficent influence without power of control.

In 1966 the following resolution was proposed to the abbots assembled in Congress: "That Anglican, Lutheran and Reformed Benedictine monks and nuns be accounted true brothers and sisters in the Holy Father Benedict." A hundred and twenty-two abbots voted in favour: one against. Such is the ecumenical spirit of Benedictines. Ever since that date the successive Abbots of our Community have been invited to attend Congresses, which now take place every four years. They share the deliberations as observers, and can be assured of a warm welcome and a ready hearing.

Benedictines are in a specially advantageous position for ecumenical work in fostering unity among Christians. For their foundation and inspiration go back far beyond the controversies which split Western Christendom in the sixteenth century, and even well beyond the schism between East and West. Benedict is still held in honour in the East. Pope Pius XI commended ecumenism to the Benedictines, desiring each Congregation to set aside one monastery or a special agent for such work. Nowadays it can confidently be said that all Benedictine monasteries of men and women are ecumenical.

The stability which Benedictines vow (see p. 66 below) provides them with a secure base from which to enter into relationships with other groups, whether within their own church or other churches – or indeed outside the Christian dispensation altogether – without feeling threatened by them. Furthermore, the family spirit which RB so strongly inculcates (see p. 36 below) makes it natural for them to embrace others in the same spirit of loving fellowship.

From its inception our Community has had its ecumenical dimension. Its very situation, in a minority as compared with the vast majority of its brothers and sisters, dictated such an attitude. Moreover, it is widely recognised that the Anglican church has long had a leading rôle in the ecumenical field. Both as Benedictines and as Anglicans we could not fail to be involved. In the years preceding World War II, our Community twice had the privilege of welcoming the Abbé Paul Couturier of Lyons, the "Apostle of Unity", whose spirit would so greatly animate the Vatican Council thirty years later. Couturier had become an ecumenist as a result of his work in aid of the impoverished Russians in Lyons, refugees from their country after the communists had come to power. This concern of his led to his becoming an oblate of the Benedictine Priory of Amay in Belgium, now at Chèvetogne, which had been founded as a result of the initiative of Pope Pius XI referred to above. It was through Amay that his ecumenical contacts were made. Subsequently our Dom Benedict Ley and Dom Gregory Dix visited him in Lyons, and, as has been said, he came twice to us. His visits widened our ecumenical vision, which had hitherto tended to look too exclusively to Rome.

Simultaneously with Couturier's visits, we were accepting for training as monks the first aspirants for what was to become our American daughter house, Saint Gregory's Priory, founded in 1939. It was established as an independent house in 1969, and is now Saint Gregory's Abbey, Three Rivers, Michigan, under its own Abbot. The Abbot and monks of Saint Gregory's experience at the hands of their Roman Catholic Benedictine compatriots the same cordial friendship as exists in England. Needless to say, there is also the warmest relationship and exchange of visits between Saint Gregory's and ourselves.

Benedictines are by no means made to pattern. There is great diversity of practice, not least in the degree of involvement with or separation from the external world. Nevertheless, they are conscious of a strong family likeness, derived from a common following of RB, however differently interpreted and lived. And this is true also of the white Benedictines, the Cistercians. And, for many years past, our Roman Catholic brethren have recognised in us also this same family likeness, indefinable, but nonetheless a profound reality.

CHAPTER FOUR:

Living the Rule

CHALLENGE

How is the Rule of Saint Benedict, written in the sixth century, to be lived at the end of the twentieth century under conditions so vastly different from those of that earlier epoch? Inevitably this presents a problem and a challenge.

For instance, Benedict says that "speaking and teaching are the master's task: the disciple is to be silent and listen" (RB 6, 6). Such was the educational method of his day, and no doubt there are times when it still applies. But today's method is different: the pupil is encouraged to speak and to question. Clearly we cannot simply go back to the past. Yet discipline of the tongue is needed in our day no less than in Benedict's.

A modern Rule can be revised as circumstances change. Such revision is impossible for us: the Rule stands. It cannot be literally observed, but the principles which it establishes must not be dis-

29

regarded. Consequently it must be re-interpreted in such a way that its spirit is preserved intact, even where the letter is set aside. Such re-interpretations inevitably vary widely. The Rule is differently applied in different monasteries. Yet such is its strength and such its wisdom and adaptability that there is a genuine family likeness among these monasteries, as was shown in the previous chapter.

A further challenge arises when a Rule written for monks is taken as a guide for those living outside monasteries: how can the Rule be lived by them? But a great deal of RB is in fact applicable to all Christians. For instance, there are few of the Tools of Good Works (RB 4) which cannot be employed with equal efficiency by oblates or by monks: indeed, for the exercise of some of them opportunities may arise more frequently in the life of an oblate than in that of an individual monk. For instance, oblates who are doctors or nurses are constantly putting into effect Tool 16, "visit the sick"; and many priest oblates have often the duty of employing Tool 17, "bury the dead."

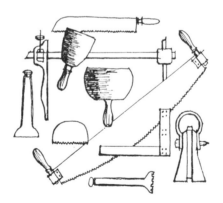

"These then," says Benedict, "are the tools of the spiritual craft" (RB 4, 75). But Benedict also devotes a chapter, RB 32, to the material "Tools and Goods of the Monastery." Such tools are to be "cared for and collected after use" (RB 32, 2). "Whoever fails to keep the things belonging to the monastery clean or treats them carelessly should be reproved. If he does not amend, let him be subjected to the discipline of the Rule." (RB 32, 4,5). Then how much more assiduous should be the care which the monk or oblate will exercise in the employment of the Tools of the Spiritual Craft! "When we have used them without ceasing day and night and have returned them on judgement day, our wages will be the reward the Lord has promised: 'what the eye has not seen nor the ear heard, God has prepared for those who love him'" (RB 4, 76,77, quoting 1 Cor. 2:9).

Faced with so imposing an array of Tools to be used, the monk and the oblate may sometimes be overwhelmed with a sense of failure in the employment of them. But Benedict is always both realistic about human weaknesses and full of tender compassion towards those who manifest them. Consequently, as the climax of his list, there comes the assurance of God's unwearying love and forgiveness. For the last tool is: "And, finally, never lose hope in God's mercy" (RB 4, 74).

Benedict's collection of seventy-two aphorisms in this chapter is a rich treasure: anyone who makes assiduous use of these tools can be assured of growth in virtue and in the love of God and man. Let us here quote three only as samples: "If you notice any good in yourself, give credit to God, not to yourself" (RB 4, 42), "but be certain that the evil you commit is always your own and yours to acknowledge" (RB 4, 43); "do not aspire to be called holy before you really are, but first be holy that you may be more truly called so" (RB 4, 62).

Benedict ends the chapter by saying, "the workshop where we are to toil faithfully at all these tasks is the enclosure of the monastery and stability in the community." The oblate, however, lives outside that enclosure and is not called to labour at the workshop bench. For her or him, therefore, the tools are not in the rack: rather their place is in the kitbag to be carried around from job to job. And the stability is not to be that of remaining in the same place, but rather in the persevering fidelity which "toils faithfully at all these tasks" (RB 4, 78).

READING THE RULE

Most modern editions and translations of the Rule are arranged for daily reading in such a way that the whole Rule is read through three times in the course of each year. Oblates are encouraged to follow this practice, so that they may be in accord with their brothers the monks. For monks, as for oblates, this means that on some days a passage is read which no longer has relevance. It has been calculated that this is true of as much as twenty per cent of the Rule. Nevertheless it is good to maintain the habit of daily reading.

There are two long sections of the Rule of which the observance is now set aside. One of these is chapters 23 to 30, the penal code which describes the punishments to be undergone by offenders, and which reflects social conditions now outmoded. The other is the long section chapters 8 to 18, in which Benedict describes in detail the arrangement of the psalms and other elements of daily worship.

In spite of the fact that Benedict allows for other arrangements, (RB 18, 22), most monasteries, including our own, adhered fairly closely to this arrangement until Vatican II. Benedict although allowing variation, as we have said, nevertheless insists that the whole psalter be recited weekly, no psalm being omitted (RB 18, 23). Today, however, practice in different monasteries varies much more widely, though all are united in regarding liturgy as the most important element in each day's work: "Let nothing be preferred to the work of God" (RB 43, 3). Our current practice at Elmore is that no psalm is omitted; every psalm is recited at least fortnightly. Making allowance for repetitions, such as at Compline, a hundred and eighty psalms are recited each week. This allows for a more frequent use of some of the more edifying psalms.

Oblates cannot undertake so much, and most of them much less; they have their individual rules in the matter. But for them also the worship of God in liturgy is a primary duty, which, in the measure appropriate to each, they perform in union with their brothers the monks.

Social conditions change, but human nature changes very little. Consequently by far the greater part of Benedict's Rule is as relevant today as it ever was, and its principles as applicable to our situation as to his. A brief summary of his spirituality was given in chapter one above, and will be expanded below. At the end of this book will be found a bibliography which will enable oblates to penetrate more deeply into that spirituality according to the capabilities and opportunities of each. Such study will enable us all to gain a deeper understanding of the Rule and a clearer vision of how we are to put it into practice.

LIFE UNDER THE RULE: LOVING GOD FIRST

Christian life, according to Benedict, is a constant encounter with God and an ever deepening relationship with Him in Christ under the influence of His Holy Spirit. It is therefore a life rooted deeply in prayer: in fact, it is prayer, if we understand that word as embracing all the activities and passivities of life, underlying and undergirding all that we do or suffer. There is nothing in life which cannot be transmuted into prayer: "every time you begin a good work, you must pray to him most earnestly to bring it to perfection" (RB Prologue, 4).

Such a relationship with God is highly personal, each of us being a unique recipient of God's love and each able to offer Him a unique love in return. None is without value in His sight. As Saint Augustine puts it, "He loves each one as though He loved that one alone."

"It is by this that we know what love is: in that Christ laid down His life for us . . . For God is love; and His love was disclosed to us in this, that He sent His only Son into the world to bring us life. The love I speak of is not our own love of God, but the love He showed us in sending His Son." (1 John 3:16; 4:9,10). Each of us has been created in love by God and redeemed in love by Christ.

Since each is so precious in the eyes of God, Benedict warns the Abbot never to undervalue the souls committed to his charge (RB 2, 31–33). Serving, as he must, "a variety of temperaments" (RB 2, 32), he must adapt his conduct towards them in such a way as to respect the individuality of each, the character and temperament, the gifts and limitations which each brings to the monastery. He must so "arrange everything that the strong have something to yearn for and the weak nothing to run from" (RB 64, 19). All of us may think that, though occasionally, by the mercy of God, we might belong to the first category, much more

34

frequently we are in the second. The respect which Benedict thus shows for the individual is reflected in the fact that each of our oblates has a personal rule of life, adapted to the particular needs and circumstances of each.

Saint Gregory says of Benedict's Rule that it is *discretione praecipua*, outstanding for its discretion. Benedict himself calls discretion "the mother of virtues" (RB 64, 19). But the Latin word is of wider meaning, including discernment as well as discretion. Because he has such discernment, Benedict's Rule is discreet: it takes account of the frailties of our human nature and is therefore gentle in its demands. Benedict will impose "nothing harsh, nothing burdensome" (RB Prologue, 46, but compare RB 58, 8). And the Abbot is to show a like discretion in exacting the obedience due to him (RB 64, 17–19).

To secure this ideal, the Abbot – and in due degree the monk and the oblate – will need that gift of the Holy Spirit which is discernment. Whether we are considering either the Rule of Saint Benedict or the personal rule of the oblate, such discernment takes account of the actual situation in which it is to be applied. Normally, the rule is the rule, and is to be obeyed for the love of God: "obedience comes naturally to those who cherish Christ above all" (RB 5, 2). But times do occur when its application would be inappropriate, or even injurious, and on such occasions it is right to abandon it. Whereas the monk in the monastery has the Abbot at hand to consult in such a case, the oblate, after brief invocation of the Holy Spirit, must decide personally: in minor matters one might even toss a coin! Should such exceptions be frequent, it may be that the rule should, with the advice of the Oblate Master, be revised or temporarily suspended.

LIFE UNDER THE RULE: LOVING THE NEIGHBOUR

Benedict is insistent on the primary place of the love of God in Christian life (RB 4, 1). He is no less insistent on the second great commandment – love of one's neighbour (RB 4, 2). In this his Rule stands in strong contrast to the Rule of the Master. RM goes so far as to say that on judgment day the only question the monk will be asked is "Have you obeyed your Abbot?" Benedict, on the other hand, would be in full agreement with Saint John of the Cross, "In the evening of our lives we shall be judged on love", love of our neighbour as well as love of God.

Benedictine life is family life. The monastery is a family in which the Abbot is father in God and the other monks all brothers. Each of them is entitled to a share in the affections of his Abbot and that of his brothers, and each is equally responsible for showing a like affection to him and to them. Consequently there must be a constant readiness for that give-and-take which is the bond of family life.

The cultivation of family virtues is therefore an integral part of the living of the Rule by the oblate, whatever be the circumstances of the life of each. Parents, brothers and sisters, spouse and children: these normally have the first claim on the affections, on the time and services of oblates – provided that the first place of all is given to loving obedience to Christ, to which "nothing whatever is to be preferred" (RB 4, 21; 5, 2; 72, 11 and compare also 69, 1,2.).

Family life, whether in the natural family or in the monastic community, is not without its difficulties and pains, hurts given and hurts received. Others have their faults, and so have we. Everyone has his or her own individual temperament, character, disposition – and idiosyncracies and fluctuations of behaviour – and it is inevitable that at times we grate on each other: "thorns of contention are likely to spring up" (RB 13, 12). Dealing with such situations is therefore an important element in living the Rule. It calls for patience and forbearance, and for a genuine and sustained effort to understand the other sympathetically and to see things from the other's point of view, "supporting with the greatest patience one another's weaknesses of body or behaviour, and earnestly competing in obedience to one another" (RB 72, 5,6).

Cardinal Hume, when Abbot of Ampleforth, in a conference to his monks gave this instruction, "Community life is made up of a lot of small things. It is the small courtesies that matter, small marks of consideration, thinking of each other, being sensitive to others, aware of their needs, tactful in handling them, kind in rebuking them, gentle". (*Searching for God*, pp. 41,42).

Before Benedict's day it had been customary for the Lord's Prayer to be recited aloud only at Mass: at other times the opening and concluding words alone were said aloud, the rest in the heart. It is because of the aforesaid "thorns of contention" that Benedict introduces the innovation of having the whole prayer recited aloud at Lauds and Vespers, so that "thus warned by the pledge they make to one another in the very words of this prayer, 'forgive us as we forgive', they may cleanse themselves of this sort of vice" (RB 13, 13). A readiness to forgive others and to seek forgiveness from them is a necessary condition for the growth of love in the monk and in the oblate: "if you have a dispute with someone, make peace with him before the sun goes down" (RB 4, 73).

There are two monastic faults against which Benedict inveighs with exceptional severity, because he sees them as destructive of the mutual love and trust which build up family life. One is what he calls "the vice of private ownership" (RB 33), which will be discussed later in this chapter. It is sufficient here to say that, clearly, any relevance that section of the Rule may have in the life of the oblate will be different from its application in the life of the monk. The other fault to receive such severe treatment is a carping, grumbling spirit: Benedict will have none of it. (RB 5, 14–19; 34, 6,7; 35, 13; 40, 9; 41, 5). Such a spirit is as inappropriate in the oblate as in the monk. But at the same time, Benedict would have the Abbot see that all genuine needs are supplied (RB 55, 18): "in this way every excuse of lacking some necessity will be taken away" (RB 55, 19, and compare also 35, 13). Nevertheless, if hardships do occur, they are to be patiently borne (RB 4, 30; 58, 3).

Happily, necessary though these warnings against dissension are, family life and social life are generally much more positive. Indeed, Saint Augustine tells us that "no surer step towards the love of God can be imagined than affection on the human level." Accordingly, Benedict would have us "respect the elders and love the young" (RB 4, 70). "To their fellow monks they show the pure love of brothers" (RB 72, 8).

Because of the importance of this mutual love Benedict would have all the brothers serve one another in the menial duties, taking them in turn a week at a time (RB 35, 1 and 6). Furthermore, each should be on the look-out for the chance of rendering voluntary service, for "obedience is a blessing to be shown by all, not only to the Abbot but to one another, since we know that it is by way of obedience that we go to God" (RB 71, 1,2; 72, 6). "No one is to pursue what is better for himself, but instead, what he judges to be better for someone else." (RB 72, 7). Oblates will find ample opportunity for putting these self-sacrificing principles into effect in their family and social life.

Courtesy is a Benedictine virtue. In various places in the Rule (RB 4, 8,23,24,70,71; 31, 13; 35, 9; 36, 3; 53, 2,3; 63, 10–17; 66, 3,4), Benedict demands from his monks that they perform towards their Abbot, their fellow-monks, their guests and all whom they encounter those small acts of courtesy, punctuality included (RB 43), which can contribute

so much to the smooth and happy conduct of social life. It is the sort of thing which Pope John XXIII called "bees' work", which cements friendships, in which he set so eminent an example. Some of the acts of courtesy which Benedict requires might today seem bizarre: nowadays monks do not prostrate themselves on the ground at the arrival of a guest! The letter of the law is abandoned, but the duties of courtesy and hospitality remain, and both monks and oblates will find opportunities of fulfilling them.

Many modern minds are puzzled by Benedict's grudging attitude to laughter (RB 4, 53,54, and the tenth and eleventh "steps of humility", RB 7, 59,60). We need to recall that he was writing in an uncouth and violent age, in which, it is reasonable to suppose, the chief occasions of laughter were the scabrous and the cruel. If that is so, his attitude is understandable, and we can so far share it. Nevertheless, we ourselves live in an age more urbane and certainly more sophisticated, in which a kindly wit and a pleasant humour can oil the wheels of social life, and keep them sweetly turning. Those then we will employ, while still being on our guard against hurting those present, or speaking ill of those absent, or drawing overmuch attention to ourselves. Nor must we take ourselves too seriously: to be able to enjoy a joke at one's own expense is a sign of grace.

Pope Gregory speaks from personal experience: "If I preserved that rigorously inflexible mode of utterance which my conscience dictates, I know that the weaker sort of men would recoil from me and that I would never attract them to the goal I desire for them. So I must frequently listen patiently to their aimless chatter." The busy Pope sets an example of patience which many oblates have opportunity to follow, especially the clergy. But is not some of our own chatter equally aimless and wide of the mark? Benedict devotes a chapter to "Restraint of Speech" (RB 6) and two of the "Tools" deal with the subject: "prefer moderation in speech and speak no foolish chatter" (RB 4, 52,53).

Community recreation was a thing unknown in Benedict's day: today it is normal Benedictine practice. At Elmore it takes place daily in the half-hour after the office of None over a cup of tea. There are also opportunities for doing one's own thing, though of course without neglect of duty.

Mutual concern and service, courtesy and hospitality: these are constructive of a civilised society and a sound social order. Benedict gives them a religious dimension. Basing himself on the words of Jesus in the parable of the Sheep and the Goats (Matthew 25:31–46), he sees such actions, especially when rendered to the neediest, as services to Christ Himself. (The sick, RB 36, 1; guests, 53, 1; pilgrims and the poor, 53, 15). Among the monk's neighbours, the Abbot holds a special, and in one way unique, place, as mediating to him the authority of Christ. It is not necessary – indeed, it would be straining after the impossible – for the monk and the oblate to remind themselves that at every such meeting they are face to face with Christ. The "sheep" and the "goats" themselves were unaware of it. Nevertheless the monk and the oblate will do well to bear in mind the aphorism of Tertullian: "You saw your brother: you saw Christ."

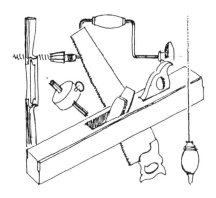

WORK

Ora et labora : "pray and work" is a Benedictine motto. Work of one sort or another occupies a large part of the normal day of the monk as also of the oblate, whether the duties be professional or domestic. There should be a harmony between our prayer life and our work life: *orare est laborare; laborare est orare.* Prayer is work; work is prayer.

As was said at the outset of this chapter, it is the aim of our life that the whole of it should become prayer. It is not for nothing that Benedict calls the divine office a work, *opus Dei.* The performance of the daily round of professional or other duties is the extension of this worship into the mundane tasks of everyday life, work becoming prayer.

The work of the monk and the work of the oblate, whether manual, intellectual, pastoral, artistic or whatever, is the staple of their service to God and their neighbour. This is still true when the beneficiary of the work is oneself. Cooking one's own dinner, for instance: it is Christ indwelling you that you so serve, and not a selfish aim. For it is your duty to maintain yourself in health and energy, so that you may the better serve God and your neighbour.

In the same sense, times of relaxation and recreation and holidays are also "the work of God", for their purpose is the same, and His blessing rests upon them. So "every time you begin a good work, you must pray to Him earnestly to bring it to perfection" (RB Prologue 4). And that includes holidays, both for monks and for oblates. For priest oblates in particular the weekly day off is an important duty.

Benedict could never have imagined what a debt the church of the future would owe to his sons and daughters, whether for their missionary and pastoral labours, or for their intellectual, educational and scholarly work. Yet the first of these two areas of work can be seen as a continuation of his own preaching to the pagans around Monte Cassino, mentioned above in chapter two, and the second as a natural outcome of his directions that a large part of each day be spent in reading (RB 48, 4,10,14,22).

To such services to the church our own community has made its contribution. To the first, in the early days, when Dom Martin Collett and Dom Bernard Clements were successively principals of Saint Augustine's College, Kumasi in what is now Ghana, and by Dom Bernard's later work as vicar of All Saints' Church, Margaret Street, London, and as a popular religious broadcaster. The two leading scholars of our community have been Dom Anselm Hughes, the musicologist, who edited *Early Medieval Music up to 1300*, which is the second volume of the New Oxford History of Music (1954); and Dom Gregory Dix, the liturgical scholar, whose chief work, *The Shape of the Liturgy*, has become a classic, still widely read after fifty years of publication.

All of this was in the unforeseeable future when Benedict wrote his Rule. He devotes two chapters to work: chapter 48, The Daily Manual Labour; and chapter 57, The Artisans of the Monastery. Such a craftsman is warned against complacency, the "feeling that he is conferring something on the monastery" (RB 57, 2). Persistence in such self-complacency, after a rebuke, earns removal from the job, until the lesson of humility has been learned (RB 57, 3).

But it is not only the craftsman who needs to be warned against self-complacency and self-aggrandisement. All those in positions of authority – and which of us, monk or oblate, is not in such a position, at least at times? – need such a warning. Not least, of course, the Abbot himself, whose "goal must be profit for the monks, not pre-eminence for himself" (RB 64, 8, a memorable, lapidary phrase in Benedict's Latin, "*magis prodesse quam praeesse.*").

The head of any department, a "dean", may be found "puffed up with pride." If he fails to amend his conduct even after three reproofs, there is nothing for it but to remove him from the job and appoint another (RB 21, 5). So too the prior is in a position of special danger of this sort (RB 65, 4).

By the very nature of their ministry, priests stand in particular need of such warnings because of other people's natural "respect for the priesthood" (RB 60, 7). So a man who is already in orders when he enters the monastery "must recognise that he is subject to the discipline of the Rule, and not make exceptions for himself, but give everyone an example of humility" (RB 60, 5).

In this chapter, Benedict makes unexpected use of words of Jesus, "Friend, what have you come for?" (Matthew 26,50; RB 60,3). They were addressed to the traitor apostle, but Benedict makes them a reminder to the priest – and to every monk and oblate – to consider constantly the purpose

43

of their vocation. It is said that Saint Bernard used to address this question to all his novices.

Benedict himself was not a priest. Elmore is exceptional among modern Benedictine monasteries in following this example and allowing the election of an Abbot who is not in holy orders. But Benedict allows for the ordination of monks in his monastery, and our practice is the same (RB 62, The Priests of the Monastery). A monk so ordained "must be on his guard against conceit or pride, must not presume to do anything except what the Abbot commands him, and recognise that now he will have to subject himself all the more to the discipline of the Rule. He must make more and more progress towards God" (RB 62, 4). Such progress is made not only by the direct service of a pastorate, but also by every form of work done to the glory of God, in whose eyes the least glamorous may be the most glorious.

"To the glory of God." It is not only a matter of what we do, but why we do it. Whatever its nature, a job well done – provided its purpose is not sinful – always tends to the glory of God the Creator. It is not necessary to be thinking of Him all the time: indeed, such thought would be impossible in many jobs which require full attention. Nevertheless, "let us open our eyes to the light that comes from God, and our ears to the voice from heaven that every day calls out this charge, 'If you hear His voice today, do not harden your hearts'" (RB Prologue 9, 10, quoting Psalm 95, 8). And in their morning prayers each day, the monk and the oblate consecrate to God the work it will include, foreseen or unforeseen: *laborare est orare:* work is prayer.

Benedict closes his chapter on the Artificers of the monastery with words which are used as another Benedictine motto, words which aptly sum up the whole purpose of the Rule: *Ut In Omnibus Glorificetur Deus*, "that in all things God may be glorified" (RB 57, 9, quoting 1 Peter 4:11).

44

THE CARE OF PROPERTY

For the individual monk, the ownership of private property is, in Benedict's eyes, "an evil practice", more literally, "a vice" (RB 33, 1). The oblate, on the other hand, will find in it an opportunity for practising virtue, a gift from God for which gratitude to Him is due. It is a responsibility in which careful stewardship must be exercised, so that it may be used in the service of God and man. That said, however, we must none of us ignore the dangers to which property exposes its owner. The warnings of Jesus to the rich are strong, clear and frequent (e.g. Matthew 6,19).

For Franciscans, poverty is a matter for a vow: it is not so with Benedictines. Since the day of Francis, the vow of poverty, along with those of chastity and obedience, has been administered in most Religious Communities in the Western Church. It has never been so for Benedictine monks, though that does not excuse them from the practice of it in their individual lives (RB 33 and 54), although its application will differ from the manner in which it is required by Francis.

Benedictines do vow stability. The obligation to stability necessitates having a permanent abode, a stable, if the monastic premises may be so described. It is a concept from which Francis, in an age later than Benedict's, but acting equally under the inspiration of the Holy Spirit, deliberately departed. Although Franciscans, like everyone else, must have places to live in, their true friary is the wide world, to which their different vocation summons them.

But Benedictine life is always local, tied to a particular place and its surroundings. Nevertheless, stability does not imply stagnation, as our own moves from Pershore to Nashdom and on to Elmore illustrate. Wherever it is, the monastery will own property, whether in the form of grounds, buildings, goods and chattels, or, nowadays in invested capital, the income from which, along with the earnings of the monks, helps to sustain the life and work of the monastery.

Following Saint Augustine, Benedict takes the practice of the primitive church as his model: "the faithful all lived together and owned everything in common: they sold all their goods and possessions and shared out the proceeds among themselves according to what each one needed." (Acts 2:44, 45, Jerusalem Bible).

Our own property is vested in the Pershore, Nashdom and Elmore Trust, a limited liability company enjoying charitable status, the income from which must, by law, be applied to the purposes set out in the Memorandum and Articles of Association of the Trust, which specify that no personal payment may be made to its members. The Board of the Trust consists of the monks in life vows, together with two nominees of the Archbishop of Canterbury, under the chairmanship of the Abbot.

Although Benedict's prohibition of private ownership by the monk does not apply to the oblate, his teaching about property in other respects is as valuable to the oblate as to the monk, although the manner of its application may somewhat vary between the two.

"The monastery should be so constructed that within it all necessities, such as water, mill and garden are contained, and the various crafts practised" (RB 66, 6). Benedict's reason for this instruction is the avoidance of unnecessary journeys outside the enclosure. For the oblate, however, the place of employment may well be at a distance from the home. (The journey, especially if it is by public transport, may offer opportunity for prayer or reading: for others, it will be the careful driving of a car which itself constitutes prayer). The main point, however, is this, that all of us, monks corporately, oblates individually, have the right to the property we need for both domestic and professional life. Similarly, Benedict lays on the Abbot the duty of ensuring that all genuine individual needs are adequately supplied (RB 34 and 55, 18) at the same time forbidding "the evil will of the envious" (RB 55, 21).

"The house of God," says Benedict, "should be in the care of wise men who will manage it wisely" (RB 53, 22). Although the spiritual progress of his monks must always be the primary care of the Abbot, that does not justify the neglect of the material welfare of the monastery. Benedict expects the Abbot to "maintain a list of the tools of the monastery" for issue and return (RB 32, 3). Today, even in a small monastery such as ours, such an inventory would be a lengthy document. Today's monk – and surely today's oblate also – puts this into practice by returning any implement to its proper place after use.

"Whoever fails to keep the things belonging to the monastery clean or treats them carelessly should be reproved" (RB 32, 4). "If anyone commits a fault while at work – whether in the kitchen, in the storeroom, in the bakery, in the garden, in any craft or anywhere else – either by breaking or losing something or failing in any other way in any other place, he must at once come before the abbot and community and of his own accord admit his fault" (RB 46, 1–3). In the monastery, such petty faults are reported at a daily meeting – and that is generally the end of it. It is salutary thus to admit one's inefficiencies! Oblates will show a like concern for their own property and behaviour, without scrupulosity about petty failures and trifling errors.

Under the Abbot's general oversight, the care of the material possessions is entrusted to the cellarer, to whom Benedict devotes a special chapter (RB 31). As they read that chapter, oblates will find material for meditation and practice in their own management of property. Above all there is a sentence which indicates forcefully how far Benedict is from drawing too sharp a distinction between sacred and secular, spiritual and material: "he will regard all utensils and goods of the monastery as sacred vessels of the altar, aware that nothing is to be neglected" (RB 31, 10,11). It is a spiritual duty to care for the material, with gratitude to God the Creator and Sustainer of all things.

Monasteries and their oblates own property. They belong to the haves of this world, in which the great majority are the have-nots. This fact puts them under obligation to do whatever lies within their power to aid their less fortunate brothers and sisters, in whom they will be serving Christ.

HUMILITY

In chapter seven of his Rule, Benedict describes Christian life as a climb up the ladder of humility. Throughout our reading of this chapter it is essential to bear always in mind the purpose of the climb, namely to take us steadily up towards the perfection of love (RB 7, 67 and compare Prologue, 47).

An alternative name for this chapter might be "The Practice of the Presence of God." For that is where it starts and that is where it ends and that is what it is all about. Though there is some progression in the twelve steps, they are not so to be understood that we only attempt the second when we believe ourselves to have mastered the first: they are all to be put into effect as occasion may serve.

Saint Augustine is another who insists on the vital importance of humility. To a young student he writes, "I want you to adopt no other means of seizing and preserving truth than that which has been put before us by Him, who, as God, has seen the weakness of our courses. And that way is firstly humility; and secondly, humility; and thirdly, humility. Not  that there are no other precepts which may be given, but unless humility precede, accompany and follow all that we do, pride would surely wrest from our grasp any good work on which we were engaged." Accordingly we must hold fast to Benedict's paradox: we descend by pride and ascend by humility (RB 7, 7).

For humility is truth: it is the recognition not only of our creatureliness but also of our sinfulness. Nevertheless, that is not the whole truth about us, for there is also good in us. That good is not to be denied, for it is the gift of God in creation: "God saw all that he had made, and it was very good" (Genesis 1:31). Consequently, the practice of humility does not demand a depreciation of the self that is precious in His eyes. "It is forbidden," says Karl Rahner, "to think meanly of the self, for that would be to think meanly of God."

Yet Benedict bids you, "Renounce yourself, in order to follow Christ" (RB 4, 10; Matthew 16:24; Luke 9:23). So it is important to have a right understanding of what is meant and what is not meant by this renunciation of the self, especially in our days when the person is so likely to be submerged in the collective. Before you can renounce the self, there has to be a self to be renounced. There must therefore be a right building up of the self as a primary duty. "As Jesus grew up he advanced in wisdom and in favour with God and man" (Luke 2:52); and so must we. The demand to deny the self is not one which is required in childhood: and which of us would claim to be fully adult and mature?

So, too, we must have a right love of ourselves. Benedict has already set before us the second great commandment, "Love your neighbour as yourself." (RB 2,2: Matthew 22:37– 39; Mark 12:30–31; Luke 10:27). There must therefore be a right love of the self as a basis for the love of neighbour.

It may seem that two of Benedict's steps of humility stand counter to the positive attitude towards the self here advocated: the sixth, "that he regard himself as a poor and worthless workman in whatever task he is given (RB 7, 49); and the seventh, that "he should be convinced in his heart that he is inferior to all and of less value" (RB 7, 51). Saints, aware of the immeasurable distance which separates them from the All-holy God, have, without affectation, so thought

50

of themselves. We lesser mortals who have not yet reached so profound a knowledge of God, may regard Benedict's sixth step as a warning against all conceit and self-complacency concerning any achievement we may attain. The seventh we may best practise by avoiding, so far as we can, comparisons altogether; and certainly those in which we compare others unfavourably with ourselves. These will be realistic ways of climbing these steps of humility and self-denial.

For there is a world of difference between the proper growth, love and affirmation of the self on the one hand, and self-complacency, self-assertiveness and selfishness on the other. "To rejoice at success is not the same thing as claiming credit for it. To deny oneself the first is to become a hypocrite and a denier of life: to permit oneself the second is a childish indulgence which will prevent one from ever growing up." (Dag Hammarskjold, *Markings*).To fish for

compliments is puerile, a sign of immaturity and insecurity: to accept them with simplicity need be no bar to humility, provided they are mentally referred to Where alone they belong. The distinction may be clear enough in theory, but for most of us it is more than a lifetime's labour to put it into practice. The ascent of the ladder of humility is a long, long climb.

But the ladder has been climbed and the summit achieved. There has been one life at least in which the self has been both totally affirmed and totally denied. For of the One who makes this demand on us, namely Jesus Himself, it can truly be said that He was, at one and the same time, the most self-affirming of men and the least selfish.

Let us heed the motive which Benedict sets before us: "Renounce yourself, in order to follow Christ" (RB 4, 10). Both in His self-affirmation and in His self-denial Christ is our model. But more than our model, for He dwells within us, transforming us into Himself by the continual action of His Holy Spirit at work in our hearts, minds and wills – yet never without our willing co-operation. It is only thus that we become our true selves, the selves we were meant to be from all eternity, the selves which we shall continue to be into all eternity.

Jesus describes this hidden action of God within us in the parable of the seed (Mark 4:26–30). "The kingdom of God is like this. A man scatters seed on the land: he goes to bed at night and gets up in the morning, and the seed sprouts and grows – how, he does not know. The ground produces a crop by itself, first the blade, then the ear, then the full corn in the ear: but as soon as the corn is ripe he plies the sickle, because harvest time is come."

It is not for the farmer to claim credit for this growth, nor indeed for the seed: it is the sunshine and rain of divine grace which have nurtured the harvest. Consequently, as Benedict says, "If you see any good in yourself, give credit to God and not to yourself, but be certain that the evil you commit is always your own, and yours to acknowledge" (RB 4, 42,43).

The ninth, tenth and eleventh steps deal with the control of the tongue, a subject on which Benedict has two Latin words at his command. He is therefore able to distinguish between the "solemn" silence which characterises the monastery at night (RB 42, 8) and the restraint of speech which should govern the day and preserve the spirit of recollection in the sight of God. In the life of the oblate, there are at least some occasions, in retreat for instance, when strict silence is appropriate and can be a constructive help. At all times all Christians should heed the severe warnings which the Epistle of James sets before us (James 3: 10–12).

There is, however, a positive reason for Benedict's insistence on silence, for it is not only, as he twice quotes from Proverbs, that "in a flood of words you will not avoid sin" (RB 6, 4 and 7, 57, Proverbs 10, 19). If the Spirit of God is to be heard in our hearts it is necessary to hush our over-busy minds, and that cannot be done if our tongues are continually on the wag. This is a truth which has its application to the spiritual progress of the oblate as well as that of the monk. For speech is a wonderful gift of God and words are therefore precious: they should be employed to his glory and the profit of his people, and not too easily dissipated.

Of Benedict's twelve steps, the fourth, patience under trials, however severe, is the steepest. It is both the most costly to climb and the one which takes us most quickly towards the summit, for it is the following of Christ all the way through. We cannot be true followers of Christ unless we are prepared to share the cross: "No man is worthy of me who does not take up his cross and walk in my footsteps" (Matthew 10:38).

His cross, let us note, not a cross, but that which is laid on him. For each of us has his or her own personal cross to carry, the particular experiences, great or small, of any kind, physical, emotional, mental, spiritual or whatever, which cause suffering to that particular person. In a way, we each of us fashion our own cross, just by being the person we are, with our own individual sensitivities. Another might think our causes of suffering trivial enough, as we might think theirs. But to all of us in one way or another, or in many ways, suffering will come: "In the world you will have trouble," Jesus warns His followers (John 16:33). And trouble there is, the world over, and we do not escape it: Jesus Himself certainly did not. Patient acceptance of the sufferings which come our way makes our cross become the cross, that which unites us to Christ crucified. His cross, no longer merely ours.

Therefore, when it comes, let us try to be uncomplaining. It is the occasion for deepening our faith and trust in God. We may not yet be able, as many of the followers of Jesus have done before us, to see our suffering as a privilege. Yet such it is, for it is a sharing of His lot and enables us to love Him more. In that spirit, Sir Thomas Browne writes in *Religio Medici*, "To be true and speak my soul, when I survey the occurrences of my life and call into account the finger of God, I can perceive nothing but an abyss and mass of mercies, either in general unto mankind or in particular to myself . . . Those which others term crosses, afflictions, judgements, misfortunes, to me who inquire further into them than these their visible effects, they both appear, and in the even have proved, the secret and dissembled favours of His affections." Many a Christian would echo Sir Thomas.

And so Benedict concludes, "Now, therefore, after ascending all these steps of humility, the monk will quickly arrive at that perfect love of God which casts out fear . . . All this the Lord will, by the Holy Spirit, graciously manifest in His workman now cleansed of vices and sins" (RB 7, 67 and 70).

PRAYERFULNESS

At the summit of the ladder of humility is perfect love. The one who has climbed it has also achieved personal maturity and unity. The whole of the life of such a one expresses one thing: God. And this has been achieved by following the one way: Christ. This following of Christ has brought about a unification of the diverse elements of the personality, such that "all that he once performed with dread he will now begin to observe without effort, as though naturally, from habit, no longer out of fear of hell but out of love for Christ, good habit and a delight in virtue" (RB 7, 68,69).

"Religion is adoration," says Baron von Hügel. Adoration forgets self and makes God the centre of life. Progress in religion is therefore a growth from self-centredness to God-centredness.

At the beginning it is inevitable – it is right – that we start from the self-centredness of babyhood. But there comes a point in the development of the child when this self-centredness begins to be ambiguous – in Christian parlance the possibility of sin arises. What was originally simple has now begun to become more complex. The self has still to be developed and affirmed: that growth must continue throughout life. But at this point a stage has been reached at which, in addition to this self-affirmation, the renunciation of self has also to become part of the process of growing towards maturity.

For the humanist, this is achieved by the practice of altruism, the principle of living for the good of others. Christians entirely agree, and can have nothing but admiration and gratitude for those who achieve it and thus serve others, ourselves often included. Nevertheless, Christians will see the humanist's underlying philosophy to be fatally flawed as a basis for human living: without religion, humanism is foredoomed to failure. This has been demonstrated before our eyes by the collapse of atheistic communism and the resurgence of religion in Eastern Europe. Such is mankind's bland unwillingness to admit its inadequacy, however, that it will doubless continue to try to live without God.

The principle of living for others is wholly accepted by Christians, but it is put into second place: the principle of living for God stands first. Benedict's Rule, in line with the whole Christian tradition, affirms this (RB 4, 1,2). His aim is that the whole of our life should become God-oriented, but this cannot be achieved without our becoming neighbour-oriented as well.

Thus the whole of our life becomes prayer, all its activities and all its passivities being united into one act of adoration. Such a unification cannot be effected without a multitude of separate acts of prayer, consecrating to God all else that we do or suffer. Therefore, says Benedict, "devote yourself often to prayer" (RB 4, 56).

It is for this reason that Benedict gives so large a proportion of each monastic day to the worship of God in the liturgy. It is the more surprising to the modern reader to discover that, in the timetables for the day in the different seasons of the year, Benedict does not include the Eucharist, even on Sundays. Nevertheless, various individual references to it (e.g. RB 31, 10; 38, 10) make it plain that the Eucharist was an important element in the life of Benedict's monastery, though we do not know how frequently it was celebrated. It is possible that, like the monks living under the Rule of the Master, those of Benedict attended a local church for its celebration, and received Holy Communion daily from the sacrament reserved in the monastery.

Certainly, however, for many centuries past the celebration of the Conventual Mass has been the most important event of every day in Benedictine monasteries, as it is in our own. So the first undertaking of the personal rules of oblates is attendance at the Eucharist, with what frequency may be possible and suitable for each. For some it may also be their only regular opportunity of corporate worship, and the more important on that account, for, "where two or three have met together in my name, I am there among them" (Matthew 18:20).

Corporate worship, whether in Eucharist or in divine office, is of central importance in the life of the monastery: "the oratory of the monastery ought to be what it is called, and nothing else is to be done or stored there" (RB 52, 1). The prayerfulness of each should contribute to the prayerfulness of all: singularity of behaviour and insensitivity to others are always out of place (RB 7, 55), but most of all here (RB 52, 3,5). For here we are, in a special sense, in the divine presence: "we believe this to be especially true when we celebrate the divine office" (RB 19, 2). A high standard of external performance is therefore obligatory, but its purpose is the nurturing of internal devotion: "let us stand to sing the psalms in such a way that our minds may be in harmony with our voices" (RB 19, 7).

All these instructions have their application to the life of oblates, even those for whom the opportunity of corporate worship is rare. In their own homes they will have their personal oratory, if not a room at least a corner consecrated to God, a focus of prayer. Although, to external appearance, they are physically alone when saying their office or meditating, they are not spiritually alone, for they are united in heart with their brothers the monks and with the whole church of God, militant and triumphant. The knowledge of this union is a source of encouragement and an incentive to perseverance. The sentry solitary on his beat is an indispensable unit of the whole army: he remains faithful at the post to which he has been assigned.

Intercession, prayer for others, is an integral part of the life of the monk. For instance, "all absent brothers should always be remembered at the closing prayer of the work of God" (RB 67, 2). Benedict is in no doubt about the power of intercession: it is the Abbot's final recourse, before expulsion, in dealing with the persistent offender: "let him apply an even better remedy: he and all the brothers should pray for him, so that the Lord who can do all things may bring about the health of the sick brother" (RB 28, 4,5).

The bidding and example of Jesus leave no room for doubt about the duty of all Christians, monks and oblates included, to offer prayer for others. Such intercession is to be seen, not as an attempt to alter God's plans, but as a strong act of faith in His love. His almighty power can and will use all things, our prayer included, to effect His saving purposes. People need praying for, and we should therefore not undervalue our prayer, feeble as we may know it to be. God values it, and uses it.

No prayer is ever wasted, even though it be not granted in the terms in which it was offered. In such circumstances, God will give, not what was asked, but, provided we persevere, much more than we have asked, for such is His nature. Perseverance is all: if an unwilling friend (Luke 11:5–8) and an unjust judge (Luke 18:2–5) can be persuaded by persistence, how much more our loving Father? (Luke 11:13). It is the teaching of Jesus Himself: "ask, and you will receive" (Matthew 7:7). Therefore "let us lay our petitions before the Lord God of all things with the utmost humility and sincere devotion." (RB 20, 2).

So "devote yourself often to prayer" (RB 4, 56). This Tool of Good Works may be put to specially effective use by the "arrow prayer" which is shot off upwards from the midst of busy occupation. Life provides many opportunities – and often an urgent need! – for such arrow prayers. It is not only at moments of crisis that arrow prayers are appropriate. Every circumstance of our life, every person we encounter, every sight which strikes our eyes, can be the occasion for darting off such an arrow: it will not fail at its mark. Let us try to build up a habit of using them; let us keep our bows at the ready – 'or, to return to Benedict's metaphor, let us keep this tool constantly handy at the top of the kit-bag, ready for immediate use at short notice.

Another large proportion of the day of the monk of Benedict's monastery was spent in reading (RB 48), especially on Sundays (RB 48, 22). Extra time was so spent in Lent (RB 48, 14–16; 49, 4). Although this extensive reading could, by natural development, produce men and women of learning, that was by no means its primary purpose. That purpose was to raise the mind Godwards. Indeed, for novices (RB 58, 5) and younger monks (RB 8, 3) a large part of this 'reading' involved committing to memory the psalms and other portions of scripture. Of such reading we might well say that if it is true that *laborare est orare*, so also *legere est orare:* to read is to pray. Such reading constitutes an important means of growth towards the love of God. Incidentally it also contributes towards the growth and maturity of the personality, for in it not only the intellect and memory, but also the emotions are involved.

Monks and oblates will do well to follow this example. Committing prayers to memory – hymns are generally easiest – provides a stock of material for use at any time, whether in a set period of prayer or as occasion may serve, for instance, when sleep is evasive. Another such opportunity may be found when doing repetitive work which does not require concentration, provided that it does not hinder the efficiency of the work, which is the primary service of God at that moment.

According to Abbot Chapman of Downside there is but one rule of prayer: "pray as you best can pray." This is in line with what Benedict says in Rule: "if at other times someone chooses to pray privately, he may simply go in and pray" (RB 52, 4). There are many people nowadays who find that they "best can pray" by the repeated use of the Jesus prayer, of which the basic form is "Lord Jesus Christ, Son of God, have mercy on me, a sinner." It may be recited in rhythm with the breathing.

A similar prayer is that with which the New Testament closes, "Amen; come, Lord Jesus!" This was, in its Aramaic form "Marana tha" (1 Corinthians 16:22), probably the earliest of all Christian prayers addressed to the ascended Lord. At that time it was a looking forward to the imminence of the end, to His final coming, but we may use it as an invitation to Him to come into our lives and the lives of all those for whom our prayers are due. For He not only will come, but comes now and comes constantly.

Orare est laborare: to pray is to work. Prayer can indeed be hard work, and it is vital not to give way to discouragement. It should not surprise us that prayer should often be difficult and seem unrewarding, for it is a reaching out towards the Infinite and the Illimitable. It seems as though, in a frail cockleshell of a boat, we were attempting to row ourselves across the ocean to an infinitely distant shore. Such a voyage would be impossible were it not for the fact that Jesus is with us in the boat. But with His companionship the success of the voyage is assured. Indeed, because of His presence with us in our boat, we are sometimes, even in this life, granted a foretaste of the joy of final arrival: "They were ready to take him aboard, and immediately the boat reached the land they were making for" (John 6:21).

For many of the people who pray regularly, most of the time it is a hard slog, plying the oars. Yet – such is their perversity! – they would not for the world be without it. Distracted mind, unresponsive heart: these are common experiences of those who voyage on the seas of prayer. Those who have travelled furthest talk of painful experiences, of dark nights of soul and spirit. To some degree we must all of us share them. The knowledge that others than ourselves – and among them the most proficient – undergo experiences like our own will encourage us to hold on in adversity. For when, to all feeling, God seems most absent, then in truth, He is most present. That truth we shall some day know by experience, but meanwhile we know it by naked faith alone. Perseverance is all.

"Nothing great was ever achieved without much enduring" (Saint Catherine of Siena). The greatest of all human achievements, the redemption of mankind, was attained by "Jesus, who for the sake of the joy that lay ahead of him, endured the cross, despising the shame, and has taken his seat at the right hand of the throne of God" (Hebrews 12:2).

We ourselves, monks and oblates, like all Christians, are engaged in something great, namely, the following of Christ in our vocation. By that vocation we are called towards the joy and the kingdom which Jesus has already gained, gained not for Himself, but for us. In our case the fulness of that joy still lies ahead. Meanwhile we have to expect that, although joy, as a gift of the Holy Spirit, is already rooted in our hearts, nevertheless our vocation will call for "much enduring." Therefore we resolve that, "never swerving from His instructions, but faithfully observing His teaching in the monastery until death, we shall through patience share in the sufferings of Christ that we may deserve also to share in His kingdom" (RB Prologue, closing words).

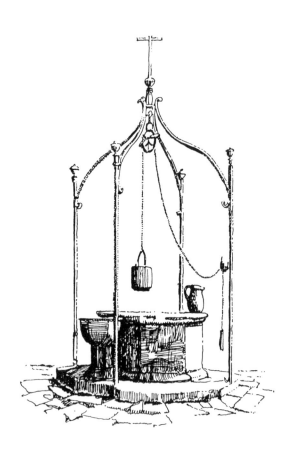

CHAPTER FIVE:

Monastic Profession and the Rite of Oblation

AS WE SAID above, Benedictines do not take a vow of poverty. No more do they vow chastity, which is simply assumed to be an integral part of the individual's commitment to monastic life.

Benedict is not unaware of the importance of the sexual urge or of the strength of the temptations to which it can give rise. According to Saint Gregory, he had personally experienced such temptations to a severe degree; and the priest Florentius had used women in his attempt to seduce Benedict's monks at Subiaco. But Benedict is by no means obsessed with the subject.

Concerning marriage Saint Paul says, ''The wife cannot claim the body as her own; it is her husband's. Equally, the husband cannot claim his body as his own; it is his wife's'' (1 Cor. 7:4). Accordingly, in the marriage service in the Alternative Service Book, at the giving or exchanging of the rings, each says to the other, ''With my body I honour you.'' Benedict speaks in similar terms of the commitment of the monk: ''well aware that from that day he will not have even his own body at his disposal'' (RB 58, 25).

Although both in marriage and in monastic profession this faithfulness has its negative aspect in the exclusion of all others from the unique relationship, yet in both cases it is undertaken for very positive purposes. Sex is God's gift to mankind: "God created man in his own image: in the image of God he created him: male and female he created them" (Genesis 1:27). By the vows of marriage and of monastic profession this gift of God is consecrated to his creative purposes, whether in the procreation of children, or in other ways, less obvious, but not less real. What that can mean in the case of the monk or nun is to be seen in the fruitfulness of the lives of the great celibate saints, men and women, and not least in Benedict himself. For by his self-consecration he has become the father of an innumerable family of sons and daughters. No wonder then that he bids us "treasure chastity"! (RB 4, 64).

At the time of monastic profession the novice, "when he is to be received comes before the whole community in the oratory and promises stability, fidelity to monastic life and obedience" (RB 58, 17). These three are not to be regarded as separate promises after the later model of poverty, chastity and obedience, but rather as one vow under three aspects.

Of these three aspects of the Benedictine vow, stability is the first and most fundamental, corresponding to the sanctity and the binding nature of the marriage vow "till death us do part." The novice, believing himself called by God to do so, thus commits himself wholly to the way of life of his monastery. For although, as was said above, stability has its local significance which is important, its significance here is much more profound, for it is a permanent committal of the self to God in the monastic way of life.

The second aspect of the triple Benedictine vow is, in Benedict's Latin, *conversatio morum*. This phrase has been the subject of wide and lively discussion in recent years, and a variety of translations have been proposed. RB 1980, from which all the quotations in this book are taken, opts for "fidelity to monastic life" (RB 58, 17). What is meant is this: that in the personal search for God – "whether the novice truly seeks God" (RB 58, 7) – which is the purpose of his entry into the monastery, the monk will persevere in using those means which are attuned to that end. For him, in particular, obedience to the Rule and to the Abbot are the principal means he must adopt. Obedience is therefore the third aspect of the triple vow.

Benedict has insisted on a thorough training beforehand – a year in the Rule (RB 58, 9–16), but it is generally agreed that a much longer period of probation is nowadays required – so that the candidate may know what he is undertaking. By now the novice has been "clearly told" – and has learned by experience – "all the hardships and difficulties that will lead him to God" (RB 58, 8). Consequently the words of the ASB marriage service are equally applicable here: "It is a way of life that all should honour, and it should not be undertaken carelessly, lightly or selfishly, but reverently, responsibly and after serious thought." It is only after such thought and earnest prayer that the novice has reached the decision to take vows: and that decision must also have been corroborated and accepted by the Abbot and chapter of the monastery in secret vote.

Like the monk, the oblate is also seeking God (RB 58, 7), and has come to believe that oblation will aid in that search. Consequently, just as for the monk so also for the oblate there has to be a period of probation, as was described in our first chapter. Its purpose is that the oblate should have learned by experience what is being undertaken, and that the Abbot and chapter may be assured of the stability of purpose of the oblate.

Oblation is an act clearly distinguished from monastic profession, yet similar to it. The oblate does not undertake the solemn vows of the monk expressed in the triple promise of stability, fidelity to monastic life, and obedience. Nevertheless, the oblate's gift of the self to God is fundamentally the same, and in both cases the gift is deeply rooted in the universal Christian grace of baptism.

Both monastic profession and oblation are to be seen as springing and developing from this root. The promises taken in these two rites are particular forms in which the original baptismal promises are to be worked out in the lives of the monk and the oblate. Consequently there will be strong resemblances between monastic profession and oblation, and both will bear a resemblance to the rite of baptism.

Monastic profession takes place in the presence of the Abbot and monks at the Conventual Mass of the monastery, following the intercessions. So too does oblation. As at baptism, after invocation of the Holy Spirit, the rites begin with questions to the candidate, the answers to which will guarantee that there is an understanding of the rite and an intention to fulfil the obligations being undertaken.

The candidate for monastic profession or oblation has beforehand written out a document stating the promise to be made. "The novice writes out this document himself . . . and lays it on the altar" (RB 58, 20), after reading it aloud and signing it on the altar. The oblate novice does the same.

The form of oblation in current use at Elmore is as follows:

"Peace!

In the name of our Lord Jesus Christ. Amen.

I, N.N., offer myself to Almighty God, asking the prayers of our Blessed Lady and our Holy Father Benedict, as an oblate of the monastery of Our Lady and Saint Benedict at Elmore, and I promise, before God and all the saints, the life of oblation, according to the spirit of the Rule of our Holy Father Benedict and the state of life to which I am called, and in the service of God and all His people."

This document the oblate signs and leaves on the altar, where it will stay till the end of the Eucharist, after which it is kept in the archives of the monastery.

"After he has put it there, the novice himself begins the verse 'Sustain me, O Lord, as you have promised, and I shall live; and do not disappoint me in my hope' (Psalm 119:116). The whole community repeats the verse three times and adds 'Glory be to the Father'" (RB 58, 21,22). This same verse, though without repetition, is said by the oblate after the signing of the document. Whether on the lips of the monk or those of the oblate, it is a confident act of trust in the grace of God for the fulfilment of what has just been undertaken.

The rite of oblation concludes with the Abbot's public reception of the oblate: "I, N.N., Abbot of the Monastery of Our Lady and Saint Benedict at Elmore, accept your oblation and admit you into full membership of our confraternity, in spiritual union with the monks, so that you may share, according to your vocation, in our life and worship."

Finally the oblate receives the Abbot's blessing and the eucharistic action is resumed, the oblate receiving Holy Communion alongside the monks.

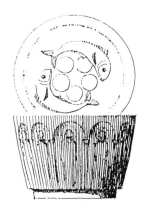

APPENDIX ONE:
Elmore Abbey

A. TIMES OF COMMUNITY MASS (LIABLE TO REVISION)

On *Sunday*, the Community attends the Parish Mass at St. Mary's, Speen, at 10.30 a.m.
Thursday, normally after Vespers at 6 p.m.
Friday, normally at 11.45 a.m.
Other weekdays, after Lauds at 8 a.m.

B. CONFRATERNITY PRAYER, said daily before Compline for all oblates, and others associated with the Community.

Abbot: Let us pray for our confraternity.

For those in pain or sorrow:	*Mother of Jesus, pray.*
For those in doubt or fear:	*Mother of Jesus, pray.*
For all clergy:	*Mother of Jesus, pray.*
For all monks and nuns:	*Mother of Jesus, pray.*
For our absent brethren:	*Mother of Jesus, pray.*
May all who honour you:	*Know the power of your prayer.*
Holy Benedict, Father of monks:	*Pray for us and for everyone.*
Turn us again, O Lord, God of Hosts:	*Show us your face, and we shall be whole.*

Stir up, O Lord, in your Church, the spirit which fired the heart of our blessed Father and Abbot Benedict, that we, being filled with the same, may learn to love what he loved, and put into practice what he taught.

Grant us, O Lord, we beseech you, to be steadfast in the service of your will, that your servants may grow in number and holiness; through Christ our Lord. *Amen.*

C. FORM OF RENEWAL OF OBLATION.

Come, Holy Spirit* fill the hearts of your faithful people, and kindle in them the power of your love.

V. Send forth your Spirit, O Lord:
R. And renew the face of the earth.

(Pause for silent prayer)

God our Father, let the Spirit you sent on your Church to begin the preaching of the Gospel, and later to fire the heart of our Holy Father Benedict, work unhindered in the hearts of your servants, and bring forth plentiful fruit in their lives. We ask this through our Lord Jesus Christ, your Son, who lives and reigns with you and the Holy Spirit, one God, for ever and ever. *Amen.*

Peace.

In the Name of our Lord Jesus Christ. *Amen.*

I renew my oblation/ and offer myself to Almighty God/ to the Blessed Virgin Mary and to the Holy Father Benedict/ and do promise before God and all the saints/ the life of oblation/ according to the spirit of the Rule of our Holy Father Benedict.

Receive me, O Lord, as you promised, and I shall live/ and do not disappoint me of my hope.

(The section between [ ] is omitted when the rite takes place during Mass).

[V. Lord, have mercy.
R. Christ, have mercy.
V. Lord, have mercy.

(Altogether)
Our Father, who art in heaven; hallowed be thy name; thy kingdom come; thy will be done, on earth as it is in heaven. Give us this day our daily bread. And forgive us our trespasses as we forgive those who trespass against us, and lead us not into temptation, but deliver us from evil. *Amen.*

V. Lord, save your servants;
R. They put their trust in you.
V. Lord, show them your love;
R. Grant them your saving help.
V. The Lord be with you:
R. And also with you.]

Let us pray for the grace of perseverance.

(Pause for silent prayer)

Everlasting God and loving Father, you know the weakness of our human nature; strengthen your servants with your abundant blessing; grant them the grace of perseverance in the promise your guidance has moved them to make by a holy and devout life, that by keeping it they may win through to everlasting life. Hear us, Father, for the sake of Jesus Christ our Lord. *Amen*

The peace and blessing of God Almighty, the Father, the Son and the Holy Spirit, descend on you and remain with you always.

Amen.

Calendar of Benedictine Saints observed at Elmore

January

12 *Benedict Biscop*, 690, abbot and founder of Wearmouth and Jarrow in Northumberland, a great collector of books. He is secondary patron of the English Benedictine Congregation.

15 *Maurus* and *Placid*, sixth century, young monks of Benedict mentioned in *Dialogue II*.

19 *Wulstan*, 1095, monk and bishop of Worcester, the only Anglo-Saxon to retain his see after the conquest: p. 24.

20 *Robert*, 1111, *Alberic*, 1109, and *Stephen*, 1124, abbots and founding fathers of the Cistercians, whose basic document, the Charter of Love, was composed by Stephen, an English monk, third abbot of Citeaux: p. 24.

February

10 *Scholastica*, c. 547, sister of Benedict: p. 14.

11 *Benedict of Aniane*, 821, abbot: p. 22.

March

9 *Frances of Rome*, 1440. With an ailing husband and several children to care for, she undertook many charitable tasks, especially in epidemics of plague. Aided by Olivetan Benedictines, she established a society of like-minded ladies. She is patron of women oblates.

21 *Our Holy Father Benedict*, c. 547.

April

21 *Anselm*, 1109, archbishop of Canterbury and doctor of the church: p. 24.

22 *Blessed Maria Gabriella of Unity*, 1939. Born in Sardinia in 1914, she entered in 1935 the Cistercian monastery of Grottaferrata, which, through the 'apostle of unity', the Abbé Paul Couturier (p. 27), was in touch with our community. Inspired by Couturier's appeal for prayer, and with the permission of her superiors, she offered her life to God as a sacrifice for unity. Stricken almost immediately by tuberculosis, she endured her pains with fortitude, not unmixed with a dash of humour. She died on St. George's Day, 1939, which was also Good Shepherd Sunday. She was beatified by Pope John Paul II in the Week of Prayer for Christian Unity, 1983. We remain in friendly contact with her community, now at Vitorchiano.

24 *Wilfrid*, 709, bishop and missionary, propagator of RB.

May

11 *Odo*, 942, *Majolus*, 984, *Odilo*, 1049, *Hugh*, 1109, and *Peter the Venerable*, 1157, abbots of Cluny in France, the most influential of Benedictine monasteries through two centuries, which made many foundations.

19 *Dunstan*, 989, *Ethelwold*, 984, and *Oswald*, 992, the friends who restored monastic life in Anglo-Saxon England: p. 24.

25 *Bede the Venerable*, 735, doctor of the church and historian, the most learned man of his time in the West, and finest flower of early Anglo-Saxon monastic life.

27 *Augustine of Canterbury*, c. 605, archbishop and apostle of the English. He is principal patron of the English Benedictine Congregation: p. 21.

June

5 *Boniface of Crediton*, 755, bishop and martyr, apostle of Germany: p. 22.

19 *Romuald*, 1027, abbot, founder of the Camaldolese Benedictines.

23 *Etheldreda* of Ely, 679, *Mildred* of Minster in Thanet, c. 700, abbesses, and all *holy Anglo-Saxon nuns*.

July

11 *Solemnity of our Holy Father Benedict*, who was proclaimed Patron of Europe by Pope Paul in 1964. Oblate Day at Elmore takes place on the Saturday next after the Solemnity, p. 7.

12 *John Gualbert*, 1073, abbot and founder.

13 *Henry*, 1024, emperor and friend of monks, who, with his wife Cunegund, was a zealous supporter of Benedictine monasticism. He is patron of men oblates.

August

20 *Bernard*, 1153, abbot and doctor of the church, the most influential churchman of his day, to whom is largely due the rapid spread of the Cistercians, p. 24.

September

3 *Gregory the Great*, 604, pope and doctor of the church, apostle of the English, author of *Dialogue II*: pp. 11 and 21. Patron of Saint Gregory's Abbey, Three Rivers, Michigan: p. 27.

October

19 *Frideswide*, c. 735, abbess, patron of the City and University of Oxford.

November

This is the month for *renewal of oblation*, either at a group meeting, p. 8, or privately at Elmore or elsewhere: Appendix I, c.

5   Commemoration of *all departed oblates, relatives and friends* of the community. Requiem Mass.

7   *Willibrord*, 739, Northumbrian, missionary, bishop of Utrecht in Holland.

17   *Gertrude the Great*, 1302, and *Mechtilde*, 1298, nuns and teachers of prayer.

20   *Edmund*, 869, king and martyr, not a Benedictine saint, but the patron of our friends and neighbours the monks of Douai Abbey.

78

APPENDIX THREE:
Books for further reading

RB 1980, THE RULE OF ST. BENEDICT in Latin and English with notes, edited by Timothy Fry, published by the Liturgical Press, Collegeville, Minnesota, USA, and available at Mowbrays, pp. 627, is an invaluable compendium of international scholarship up to the fifteenth centenary of Benedict's birth and is essential for study in depth. It is also published in an abridged form, including the notes and thematic index, pp. 196. This translation of RB is also separately published in pocket size, and is handy.

Three classics, older books in which some of the material is dated but whose value persists:

COMMENTARY ON THE RULE OF SAINT BENEDICT, Paul Delatte, 1920, pp. 501, a magisterial work by the Abbot of Solesmes, France;

BENEDICTINE MONACHISM, Cuthbert Butler, 1919, pp. 388, a profound, yet popular exposition of Benedictine life by the Abbot of Downside;

CHRIST THE IDEAL OF THE MONK, Columba Marmion, 1926, pp. 463, shows the strongly Christocentric nature of Benedictine spirituality.

More recent scholarship is ably displayed in two books by Adalbert de Vogüé:

COMMUNITY AND ABBOT, two vols., pp. 256 and 506, and:

THE RULE OF SAINT BENEDICT, pp. 403, both published by Cistercian Publications and available through Mowbrays.

Less intellectually demanding but also instructive are the following four:

HOUSEHOLDS OF GOD, David Parry, DLT, 1980, pp. 199, a translation and commentary on the Rule with explanations for monks and laypeople today;

THE WAY TO GOD, Emmanuel Heufelder, Cistercian Publications, 1983, pp. 297, reflections on RB by a German Abbot.

A SHARE IN THE KINGDOM, Benet Tvedten, Liturgical Press, Collegeville, pp. 142, written for American oblates;

THE RULE OF BENEDICT, Gerard MacGinty, Dominican Publications, Dublin, 1980, pp. 166, "Themes, Texts, Thoughts on the Rule," pocket-size.

Of primary importance as expositions of Benedictine spirituality today are:

CONSIDER YOUR CALL, ed. D. Rees, SPCK, 1978, pp. 447, which takes a fresh look at the principles in the light of contemporary issues of universal concern.

SEARCHING FOR GOD, Hodder and Stoughton, pp. 239. Cardinal Basil Hume, when Abbot of Ampleforth, gave instructions to his monks which can shed much light on the daily endeavour of all Christians.

How widely Benedictine spirituality appeals and applies is demonstrated by the acclaim given by the general public – and no less by monks and nuns – to Esther de Waal's:

SEEKING GOD, Collins Fount, 1984, pp. 160. She has followed this up with:

LIVING WITH CONTRADICTIONS, reflections on the Rule of St. Benedict, Collins Fount, pp. 164. Mrs de Waal commends "for its wonderfully practical presentation" a more recent book by another Anglican priest's wife, Norvene Vest, Oblate OSB:

PREFERRING CHRIST, published by Anthony Clarke, 1990, pp. 174, a devotional commentary and workbook on RB.

A further selection of relevant literature is given in:

THE BENEDICTINE LIFE, Recommended Reading, 1990, pp. 26, available from the Oblate Master, Ealing Abbey, London W5 2DY.